My coffee table

Myra Rao

Presentation by *BookLeaf Publishing*

Web: www.bookleafpub.com

E-mail: info@bookleafpub.com

ISBN: 9789357745062

First edition 2023

To Dad,

My hero, my inspiration and my role model

Everything I am is all because of you 🩶

PREFACE

All those bright and sunny days,
All those bleak and sleepless nights,
All those sweet and soft memories,
And all those bitter and tougher lessons
....have led to this
May be a small step, but represents a giant leap
forward

Planet Plato

I guess in this day and age,
when most of us are looking for love and
embrace,
We all forget those we have right around the
corner, those who love and treat us with utmost
honor

There is that person who buys you a midnight
strawberry shake
There is that pal who listens through your 4-hour
call full of rage

There is also that buddy who gets on that plane
to be with you in your worst quake
There is this one too who holds your hand
through life's toughest stage

This is a love letter to all those folks divine
I am proud that I get to say you are all mine
All these years turned into a lifetime
And all of a sudden, you've become my lifeline

Primordial, eternal and adaptable,
Platonic love is the love that is very much
palpable!

To the one that's gone but lives on

I can't leave it in my mind,
And I can't bury it in the earth.
So I carve these words off my heart,
And hope that one day, someone
Looks at my pain and calls it art

I wish I had stopped losing you,
Or I could stop losing my mind over you
I wish I could be normal
But my heart is sick and longs for you

All I am left with is the beautiful memory that is
your life,
And the gaping void of your absence in this
silent grief

And to everyone who asks me why I sleep a lot,
How can I explain that dreams are the only place
where I get to see you and interact?
May be I could see you one more time walking
through that door,
Alas! Reality kicks in that I can never hear your
voice anymore

I know you don't want me to cry,
But if you can ever feel my tears, can you please
come by?

They say that the life we continue to live on
Will be flowers to put on their grave
I could only hope and lead mine in a way
That would put yours in a cherry blossom
garden, so brave

Diaspora: To all my fellow people living outside of their homeland

In lands both near and far away,
The people from their homes did stray
For reasons great and reasons small,
They left behind their cherished walls

And so they traveled far and wide,
To lands where they could hope to reside
And build a life that they could call
Their own, with dreams both big and small

But though they left their homelands behind,
Their hearts and souls remain aligned
With all they loved and all they knew,
Their culture, customs, and roots so true

For diaspora is not just a place,
But a journey that they must embrace
With courage, hope, and resilience
To build a new life with great brilliance.

Leaving crumbs of you

I look at all those packed boxes,
and all those empty closets,
all the empty rooms,
reminiscent of mysterious doom

The places where memories were made,
the corners where friendships were braided,
the pillows that saw muffled cries,
and that kitchen with chips and fries

Isn't it marvelous to think that we leave pieces
and parts of us
whenever we leave a house we called home for a
while,
and move on with new memories and a wee-bit
transformed selves,
not to forget the new mementos and souvenirs
with a smile?

I look at all those boxes,
which got rid of old 'stuff' that once meant so
much,
all those empty closets,
that were once filled with everything of my
touch

All of those empty rooms once carried my life,
my work, my late-night singing, my stupid
dances and tales awkward,
but knowing that I take a part of this place with
me as I fly,
I stride along to leave my mark at another place,
up and onward

Unlived and Untested love

Can't say why
Can't say how
But when I think about you
All I feel is "safe" and "home"

'Cause hope resembles a lot like your name
A lot like your laughter and
A lot like you

But you never knew what truly it could have
been,
Nor did I
Standing alone in the plastic mirror
Stuck between "I really want to talk to you" and
"I really want to get over you"

Maybe you have been in it all along, but for you,
it was easier to runaway
With all the things left to say

Now I swim in an ocean of regret
With the skeleton of your ghost
Leaving behind a galaxy of tears for every
embrace
I couldn't hold on to
Buried in the cemetery of my soul

My only takeaway?
I love those parts of myself harder,
The parts that you refuse to choose!

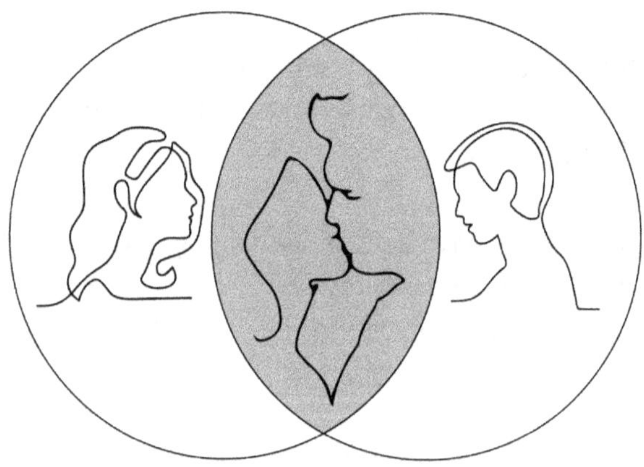

My sunsets

The waves roll in, in a soothing hum,
As the sand tickles my toes, and the salty air fills
my lungs
The sea stretches out before me,
Endless waves of blue
The sand a canvas to the beauty,
A place where dreams come true.

The sun sets, in a golden blaze,
And the world around me is a peaceful haze.
As the day turns to night, and the stars light up
the sky,
The beach and the sea, remain a sight for the eye

So I'll sit here, on this shore so serene,
And let the sea and the sand, wash over me
For in this moment, I feel free,
And I know, this is where I'm meant to be.

Blue Lava

She is sick of being told, to be seen and not
heard
To take what she's given, and not utter a word
To smile and nod, to be polite and nice
To put up with the abuse, and not to think twice

For too long, she has been kept in chains
Invisible shackles, that caused her pain
But no more, she refuses to be oppressed,
She'll stand up and fight, and do her best

She's got a voice, and it's time to be heard
To speak her truth, and not be deterred,
To let out the rage that's been suppressed
It's time to harness, this burning flame

There she goes -

"So hear me now, and hear me well,
I'm breaking free, from this living hell,
I'll rise above, and claim my place,
For my anger is the fuel of my grace."

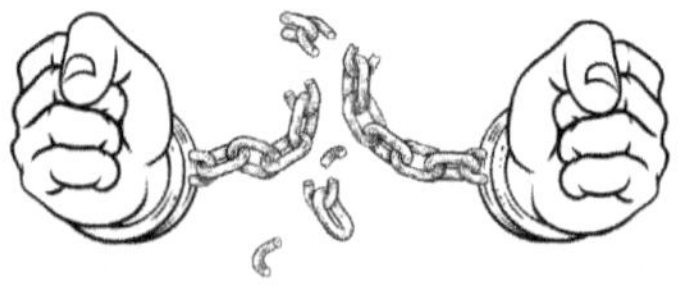

Hope in the Shadows

Are we always where the light is?
Or sometimes we just stand in the shadows and
wonder why?
Those shadows that lurk around,
those that tell us that everything is wrong

That darkness that looms around,
and tells us that we are worthless,
or no one can help us,
Drowning in the silence that's so loud,
questioning everything we ever knew,
or even the mere existence

But what if I tell you that
whatever you are searching for,
is on the other side of difficult emotions?
That there is hope waiting for you in the dark,
That little glimmer of sunshine,
waiting for you to touch it and embark

There's the old you, the original you,
or the other you,
loitering on the other side of this tunnel,
the only way out is through

Maybe you are just two steps away
from the dreaded path to the end,
doubting if you could ever make it,
But I know you will and you can

You will do it because it must be done,
You will do it because no one else can,
When the world deals its cards,
you can always show your best game

Can you give people around you a chance?
'Cause sometimes support comes from the rarest
of places,
Love shows up at the rarest of occasions

Can you be a dearie and do me a favor?
Please show the planet what a miracle you are!

Thank you, next!

It's easy to get lost in the noise,
Of other people's thoughts and desires
But your heart and your soul are your choices,
And only you can light your own fires.

For you are unique, a one-of-a-kind soul,
With gifts and talents, all your own
And you have the power to take control,
Of your own path, and make it known.

Do not let others dim your light,
Or make you feel less than you are
For their words and actions are not so bright,
And they cannot steal your inner star

You are the one who knows your heart,
And what makes your soul truly smart
You are the one who has the power,
To create a life that's truly yours

Remember, you are not a consequence of other's opinions,
But a unique individual with your own visions
So be brave, be bold, and be true,
And let your own light shine through.

2AM thoughts

That feminine urge to pretend a "drunk/high
call"
With that guy you miss but won't admit
So you go back online and dig it all
All those chats that failed to continue after you
fell adrift

And then I wonder,
Have you ever lain on the bed wide awake at 2
am,
Searching so intensely in the depths and realms
of your brain,
Your memories and your heart, for something
that you already know the answers to?
Do you remember how it feels?

Well, it leaves a pathetic state of mind,
A bitter taste on the tongue
Weariness in the eyes, and a stab in the heart,
Fresh in experience.

Love Letter

It takes a lot of bravery to walk away,
From someone who once held your heart
To break free from the cycle of dismay,
And make a brand new start.

You faced the fear, the guilt, the shame,
And spoke your truth, despite the blame.
You stood up for your dignity,
And refused to be a victim of toxicity.

I know it must have not been easy,
And that you must have had many fears
But you took that step, day by day,
And overcame your doubts and tears.

You deserve love, respect, and kindness,
And a life free from fear and pain
And though the scars of the past may still
remind us,
Your future holds promise, sunshine, and rain.

So hold your head up high, my dear,
And know that you are loved and supported
And that your courage and strength are crystal
clear,
A testament to the resilience you've imported.

Cupcakes of kindness

In this world, so full of pain
Let kindness and love, be our main gain
For in every heart, there is a spark
That needs only love, to light up the dark.

Be kind to the stranger, that you meet on the
street
And offer a smile, to the one you might greet
For a simple gesture, can go a long way
And brighten someone's day, in a remarkable
way.

Be loving to the earth, that we all call home
And let her breathe, and freely roam
For the trees, the rivers, and the skies
Are all part of us, and deserve to thrive.

Be kind and loving to yourself
And treat yourself, with kindness and wealth
For you are a part of this world, so precious and
true
And you deserve love, in all that you do.

Let us spread love, and kindness around
And let our hearts, be the loudest sound
As in this world, so full of strife
Love and kindness are the keys to a better life.

Pancakes on a Sunday morning

In a quiet home, with love and light,
Lived a couple, whose bond was tight
They woke up each morning, with a smile,
And went about their day, without a trial.

He made her coffee, just the way she liked,
And she packed his lunch, with love so spiked
They kissed each other, before they left,
With a promise, that they would not be bereft.

They were lost in their worldly daily chaos
throughout the day,
But they always came back home, their home in
each other
They went on walks and they held hands,
And talked about life, its ups and its bends.

At night, they cooked together, with glee,
And watched movies, snuggled up, just then and
there
They laughed, they cried, they hugged and
kissed,
And thanked the heavens, for this perfect bliss.

And though life may not always be this way,
And troubles may come, on some fateful day,
This couple knew, that love was their glue,
And together, they could make it through.

For in each other, they had found,
A love so true, so pure, and so sound,
That nothing could break it come between
This couple, whose love, was a perfect scene.

So one Sunday, you are going to wake up
Next to this person who makes everything look
fine,
And you both are going to cuddle in the kitchen
so wide,
Making pancakes and living the life from the
above lines

The girl in Italic font

She sits in the corner, lost in a book,
Her glasses perched on her nose, with a studious
look
She's quiet and shy, but with a heart so pure,
And a mind so brilliant, that it could endure.

She loves to read, and learn new things,
And writes in her journal, with thoughts that
sing
She's a lover of science, math, and art,
And believes in the power of a curious heart.

Her softness is a shield, she wears it with pride,
For she knows that her heart can never be denied
She may seem meek, a bit shy,
But her inner strength never runs dry
She dances till her feet get numb,
sings and croons to you a sweet melody,
Oh, careful, she might also blow you away with
her love for movies,
but can still go on for hours about all things
political and sporty

She's the kind of girl, who'll listen to your woes,
And offer a kind word, that's soft as a rose

She'll lift you up, when you're feeling low,
And show you the way, to let your heart glow.

So don't overlook, this nerdy soft girl,
For she's a gem, that could make your world
swirl,
With her intellect, and her kind-hearted soul
She's the kind of girl that could make you whole.

Chasing butterflies

Unleash your inner child, let it be free
Throw away the shackles, and just be
Let go of the worries, and the strife
And step into a world full of life.

Play in the rain, jump in the puddles
Dance to the beat, and forget all the muddles
Sing at the top of your lungs
And let your spirit burst with joyful songs.

Draw on the walls, and paint with your hands
Build a sandcastle, and let your imagination
expand
Run in the fields, and chase the butterflies
And feel the joy that never really dies.

Laugh till your belly hurts, and your eyes are
wet
And let your heart feel lighter than a feathered
pet
Remember the days when life was just fun
And bring back the child that was long gone.

For in this world of responsibilities and stress
We often forget, the child we once did possess

But it's never too late to loosen up and play
And bring back the child in a joyful, colorful
way.

Young Love - Things left unsaid

I remember the days, of my teenage years,
When crushes were simple, and free from any
fears
The butterflies in my stomach, when they passed
by,
The racing of my heart, as they caught my eye.

Let me take you through that ride,
All the sweet things that you are guilty of
but can never deny

You see them every day, and your heart skips a
beat,
Your cheeks turn red, and you can barely speak
You want to tell them, how you feel inside,
But the words, they just won't come out right.

They make you smile, with just a passing
glance,
And every time, you get lost in a trance
You try to hide, these feelings you have for
them,
But they just keep growing, and you don't know
what to do.

You would daydream of them in the middle of
class,
And write their name, on your notebook with a
heart made of glass
You would listen to love songs, and think of
them,
And wonder if they ever felt the same way too.

Do you remember the thrill of their brief
conversations?
And how you replayed them, in your mind with
elation
The way they smiled, and the way they spoke
Left you breathless, with a heart full of hope.

But as the years passed, we went our separate
ways,
And the memories of our crush, started to fade
away,

For even though, we never took that chance,
And our crushes remained, a simple romance,
I will always cherish, the memories we had,
And the way they made me feel, when I was just
a teenage kid.

That Friday night in the city

Have you seen those three girls,
singing and swaying,
perfectly in bliss,
nothing in the world bothering?

They look so happy,
chattering and giggling,
it's hard to tell them apart
from the lights of the city
as they continue their curbside dancing

I'm sure you slightly judged them,
or just gushed at how happy they are,
and secretly wondered how it would be
to be one of them or to have a night like that

Yes, I AM one of them,
just swooning over my friends and I,
never realizing this is how my thirties can be,
and being single isn't boring or a crime

It's never too late to take charge of life,
to try the things that you never dared
Enjoy the little things this world has to offer,
the judgements and misconceptions not to care

It's these simple things and innocent nights
that matter the most when you look behind
We are making memories and filling the void
when the world is sleeping in its ignorant trite

Twin Peaks - night under the stars

I gaze up at the sky,
And marvel at their dazzling display
Their shimmer and sparkle, oh my,
A universe so vast and far away.

In love with the stars, I am,
A cosmic dance, a divine program
I wonder at their stories untold,
Of black holes and mysteries bold

And then I bow down to see the world under my
feet
The city lights, a glittering sea,
Of neon signs and traffic streams
A vibrant pulse of energy,
A city's heart, bursting at the seams.

Lights and stars, a dazzling display
In the sky and on the earth below
A symphony of shimmer and sway
A magical dance, both fast and slow.

The lights and stars, they interplay
A canvas of beauty, so diverse
A waltz of color, a grand ballet
A masterpiece of art and verse.

The world outside my
window pane

The rolling hills, the winding roads,
The changing landscapes, a sight to behold.
The sky above, a canvas of blue,
With clouds like cotton candy, fluffy and true.

The music plays, a steady beat,
We sing out loud and tap to the beat
The wind in our hair, the stars on our face,
We share our thoughts and dreams
As we cruise down the open road
Our souls are free, our hearts light,
And our spirits are unburdened and bold.
The miles slip by with ease,
As we lose ourselves in the drive,
The long road ahead is our canvas,
And this journey is the ultimate prize.

For on long drives, we discover,
A part of ourselves we didn't know,
As we let the road guide us,
And let our hearts and souls slow.

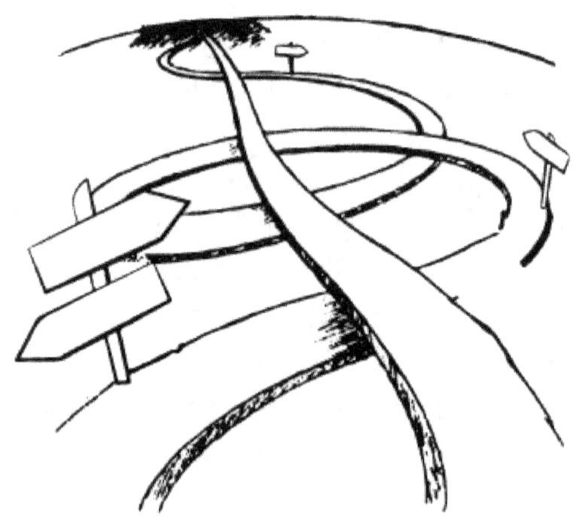

A Song for the soul

Like a gentle breeze in the early dawn,
Like a soft wave touching the feet on,
Like the warm hug on a cold long day,
Music speaks in many different ways

There's a song that evokes sealed memories,
A song that could gently put me to sleep,
Oh! A song reminding me of that summer night,
Another one for a rainy day to hold on tight

Don't you have a song to lift your spirits up
high?
Or the tune that can make you feel that you are
ready to conquer the universe?
I know you love a sound that makes your feet
jump and fly,
And we all have one that reminds us of that lost
love bliss

From the beat that pulses in our veins
To the melody that soothes our pains,
Music touches every part of us
And helps us feel both joy and trust

It can make us laugh or make us weep,
It can give us comfort when we're deep
In sorrow or in strife and pain,
Music helps us feel whole again

So let us listen to its voice,
And let its power be our choice,
To help us face each day anew,
And find the strength to follow through.

Down the memory lane

Walking down the streets I used to know,
The memories come rushing like a sudden blow
I am back to where I was born,
And all the feelings, I thought were gone.

The air smells of nostalgia and home,
And I feel like I am no longer alone
The streets, the people, the sights and the
sounds,
All of it brings back what I thought was lost and
never to be found.

The park where we used to play,
The school where we learned every day,
The shops and the restaurants we used to
frequent,
All of it brings back memories so vivid and
vibrant.

The people, the friends that I left behind,
Are still here, etched in my mind
Their faces, their smiles, their laughter,
Are all back, like a happy ever after.

I feel a longing for the times that were,
For the people I loved and cared for,
But I know I cannot go back in time,
And the past is just a memory that will never be
mine.

But as I walk down the streets of my hometown,
I know that a part of me will always be bound
To the memories and the moments that we
shared,
And the love that we had, that we once paired.

I do wonder if this is how it was,
The streets once wide and spread afar now
looking so small,
Did I outgrow my hometown,
Or that kid was so tiny that she felt everything
was so big and tall?

So, I embrace the nostalgia that I feel,
And cherish the memories that are so real,
For they are a part of me, and I of them,
And I know that in my heart, they will never
end.